SAM SHEPARD

Kicking a Dead Horse

Sam Shepard is the Pulitzer Prize–winning author of more than forty-five plays. He was a finalist for the W. H. Smith Literary Award for his story collection *Great Dream of Heaven*, and he has also written the story collection *Cruising Paradise*, two collections of prose pieces, *Motel Chronicles* and *Hawk Moon*, and *Rolling Thunder Logbook*, a diary of Bob Dylan's 1975 Rolling Thunder Review tour. As an actor he has appeared in more than thirty films, including *Days of Heaven*, *Crimes of the Heart*, *Steel Magnolias*, *The Pelican Brief*, *Snow Falling on Cedars*, *All the Pretty Horses*, *Black Hawk Down*, and *The Notebook*. He received an Oscar nomination in 1984 for his performance in *The Right Stuff*. His screenplay for *Paris, Texas* won the Grand Jury Prize at the 1984 Cannes Film Festival, and he wrote and directed the film *Far North* in 1988 and cowrote and starred in Wim Wenders's *Don't Come Knocking* in 2005. Shepard's plays, eleven of which have won Obie Awards, include *The God of Hell*, *Buried Child*, *The Late Henry Moss*, *Simpatico*, *Curse of the Starving Class*, *True West*, *Fool for Love*, and *A Lie of the Mind*, which won a New York Drama Desk Award. A member of the American Academy of Arts and Letters, Shepard received the Gold Medal for Drama from the Academy in 1992, and in 1994 he was inducted into the Theatre Hall of Fame. He lives in New York.

ALSO BY SAM SHEPARD

Buried Child

Tooth of Crime (Second Dance)

The God of Hell

Great Dream of Heaven

*The Late Henry Moss, Eyes for Consuela,
When the World Was Green*

Cruising Paradise

Simpatico

States of Shock, Far North, Silent Tongue

A Lie of the Mind

The Unseen Hand and Other Plays

Fool for Love and Other Plays

Paris, Texas

Seven Plays

Motel Chronicles

Rolling Thunder Logbook

Hawk Moon

Kicking a Dead Horse

SAM SHEPARD

Kicking a Dead Horse

A PLAY

Foreword by Stephen Rea

VINTAGE BOOKS

A Division of Random House, Inc.

New York

A VINTAGE BOOKS ORIGINAL, JUNE 2008

Copyright © 2007 by Sam Shepard
Foreword copyright © 2008 by Stephen Rea

All rights reserved. Published in the United States by Vintage Books,
a division of Random House, Inc., New York, and in Canada by
Random House of Canada Limited, Toronto. Originally published
in slightly different form in the United Kingdom by
Faber and Faber Limited, London, in 2007.

Vintage and colophon are registered trademarks of
Random House, Inc.

Library of Congress Cataloging-in-Publication Data
Shepard, Sam, 1943–
Kicking a dead horse : a play / by Sam Shepard;
foreword by Stephen Rea.
p. cm.
"A Vintage original"—T.p. verso.
ISBN: 978-0-307-38682-3
1. Art dealers—Fiction.   2. West (U.S.)—Drama.   I. Title.
PS3569.H394K53 2008
812'.54—dc22
2008001503

www.vintagebooks.com

Printed in the United States of America
10 9 8 7 6 5 4 3 2 1

For Stephen Rea

Special thanks to Peter Stampfel

Foreword

Three writers dominate late-twentieth-century drama: an Irishman, an Englishman, and an American—Beckett, Pinter, and Shepard.

All three are engaged in a theater that is beyond the mere traffic with, in Yeats's phrase, "the sensation of an external reality."

Beckett's method in drama depends on a sense of formal limits, so that his use of theater has been an investigation of its nature.

"When an essay in a genre is a critique of that genre and meaning expresses itself against boundaries, bridges are burnt behind the writing as it advances."★

The method opens onto a disturbing freedom and has been hugely influential. Pinter and Shepard acknowledge

★J.C.C. Mays, *Field Day Anthology.*

freely this influence on their work, and no writers have seized upon Beckett's legacy with such willingness. What Pinter found in Beckett was a writer "inhabiting his innermost self," and what impressed him was "something about the quick of the world"*—a writer creating his own unique yet universally recognizable world.

Sam Shepard felt that in the 1960s Beckett made American theater "look like it was on crutches" and that "he had revolutionized theater, turning it upside down, and making it possible to write about anything."

What Pinter and Shepard have done is to claim the Beckettian existential space and re-create it in rooms, ranches, prairies, badlands. (What is Pinter's *The Dumb Waiter* but Godot in a basement?) The characters of Pinter's *Landscape* and *Ashes to Ashes*, and Shepard's *Fool for Love* and *A Lie of the Mind*, like Hamm and Clov in *Endgame*, are doomed for eternity to petrified noncommunication.

It's a wholly nontheoretical theater. Pinter insists that he doesn't conceptualize in any way. Shepard denies starting from any kind of abstract idea or theory. Beckett said, "My work is a matter of fundamental sounds—Hamm as stated, Clov as stated—that's all I can manage" and "Godot began with an image of a tree

*Michael Billington, *The Life and Work of Harold Pinter*, (London: Faber & Faber, 2007).

and an empty stage and proceeded from there. I only know what's on the page."*

Kicking a Dead Horse begins with a description of, yes, a dead horse, stipulating that there should be "no attempt to stylize or cartoon it in any way. In fact, it should actually be a dead horse." The play begins with a concrete dramatic image and proceeds from there.

By now it's a cliché to assert that writing aspires to the condition of music. But . . .

Beckett: "Music is the highest art form—it's never condemned to explicitness."†

And to an actor (me) in rehearsal: "Don't think about meaning, think about rhythm."

The plays of Sam Shepard, more than any writer since Beckett, feel like musical experiences. They transcend meaning, avoid the literary and conceptual, and search for a concrete immediate reality, beyond the idea, which the actor and audience are forced to experience directly.

And here's the leap.

In *Kicking a Dead Horse*, we watch with some shock as Shepard dismantles the imagery that distinguishes

---

*Laurence Shainberg, "Exorcising Beckett," from *Playwrights at Work: The Paris Review*, ed. George Plimpton, (New York: Modern Library, 2000).

†Shainberg, "Exorcising Beckett."

the previous body of his work. As Hobart Struther realizes the futility of his quest for AUTHENTICITY and divests himself of the mythology that has sustained him hitherto, we experience the urgency of the wider American crisis: the collapse of a sense of history and maybe of America itself.

Beckett said of Joyce, "His writing is not about something. It is something."★

That, of course, is Sam Shepard's achievement.

—*Stephen Rea*

★Shainberg, "Exorcising Beckett."

Kicking a Dead Horse

Kicking a Dead Horse premiered at the Abbey Theatre, Dublin, Ireland, September 13, 2007.

HOBART STRUTHER:	Stephen Rea
YOUNG WOMAN:	Joanne Crawford

Directed by	Sam Shepard
Set design by	Brien Vahey
Lighting design by	John Comiskey
Costume design by	Joan Bergin
Voice direction by	Andrea Ainsworth
Dialect coaching by	Brendan Gunn
Assistant directed by	Wayne Jordan
Company stage management by	Brendan McLoughlin
Deputy stage management by	Elizabeth Gerhardy
Assistant stage management by	Róisin Coyle
Hair and make-up by	Patsy Giles
Photography by	Ros Kavanagh
Graphic design by	Red Dog

HORSE MAKERS:

Sculptors	Padraig McGoran, John O'Connor
Mechanism	Shadow Creations
Assistants	Tony Doody, Rory Doyle
Model maker	Mike McDuff

Characters

HOBART STRUTHER
mid-sixties

YOUNG WOMAN

*All stage positions (up left, up right, down center, etc.)
are from the actor's point of view, facing audience.*

Scene: as the audience enters, the stage is entirely covered with a sky-blue silk sheet concealing irregular mounds. No special lighting and no music or sound effects of any kind. A blank white muslin scrim covers the entire upstage wall in a wide sweeping arc, floor to ceiling. No special light in scrim other than work lights.

Once the audience settles, piano music begins: Dr. John's "Just a Closer Walk with Thee," track 7 from the CD, Dr. John Plays Mac Rebennack. After first short piano phrase, lights begin slowly to dim to black. This fade takes up the next long verse of the song entirely. Once the verse is completed and lights have gone down to black, the scrim begins slowly to fill with a pale straw light reminiscent of wide-open prairie at midday. As the second verse unfolds and the lights are slowly rising, the sky-blue silk sheet begins to be drawn back very slowly toward the upstage wall, revealing a dark pit downstage center with mounds of fresh earth on either side of it. Directly upstage center of the pit, on a slight rise, is a dead horse laid out on its side, spine toward audience, neck and head sprawled out to stage right, tail to stage left, all four legs stiffly toward upstage. There is no blood or sign of external injury. The dead horse should be as realistic as possible with no attempt to stylize or cartoon it in any way. In fact, it should actually be a dead horse.

Music fades out. Light is now full in scrim and stage, giving the effect of distant endless horizon in flatlands. Silence, then, from deep in the pit, the sound of a shovel piercing earth followed by the guttural exhalation of a man working hard. A spadeful of dirt flies out of the hole and lands on the mound to stage right. Slight pause, then this whole sequence repeats. Slight pause and the sequence repeats twice more, the spadefuls of earth landing on the stage-left mound. Slowly, a man emerges from the hole, appearing to the stage-right edge carrying a small camp shovel and breathing heavily. He tosses the shovel on the stage-right mound and climbs completely out of the hole. He stands there, breathing heavily, facing stage right, then bends over, exhausted, placing his hands on his knees.

This is Hobart Struther: mid-sixties, rumpled white shirt, no tie, sleeves rolled up, no hat, baggy dark slacks, plain boots for riding but not cowboy boots, dark vest. There should be no attempt in his costume to make him look like a "cowboy." In fact, he should look more like an urban businessman who has suddenly decided to rough it. Blotches of dirt and sweat cover him from head to foot. He has been digging all day. He straightens up, still trying to catch his breath, and turns back toward the hole. He stares down into the pit, then looks upstage at the horse, then directly at the audience, then back to the horse again. Each of these "looks" should be very distinct and deliberate, in the mode of the classic circus clown. He looks back at the audience.

HOBART: Fucking horse. Goddamn.

He moves downstage right, where a jumbled pile of equipment has been tossed: western saddle, horse blanket, chaps, spurs, bridle, canteen, small duffel bag full of canned beans, jerky, pots and pans, small canvas tent in the old style, bedroll, rope, saddlebags, and brand-new cream-colored western hat. All of these objects should be totally functional and plain. He starts rummaging through all the gear, searching for a pair of large black binoculars in a case, talking to himself the whole time.

(*Searching through gear.*) Of all the damn things—all the things you can think of—preparations—endless lists. All the little details, right down to the can opener and the hunk of dental floss you throw in just for the heck of it. All the forever thinking about it night and day—weighing the pros and cons—last thing in the world that occurs to you is that the fucking horse is going to up and die on you! Just take a shit and roll over like a sack of bones.

Looks at audience, motions to horse.

Look at that! Dead! Deader than dirt. There he is— deader than dirt.

He finds the binoculars in the saddlebag, takes them out of their case as he crosses to the stage-right pile of dirt and climbs to the top of it. He holds the binoculars up to his eyes and looks over the heads of his audience. As he talks to himself, he turns very slowly clockwise in a tight, 360-degree circle, keeping the binoculars to his eyes and scanning out to the horizon the whole time.

(*Scanning with binoculars.*) Now what? Nothing— nowhere—here I am—miles from nowhere. Only one day into it and bottomed out. Empty—badlands— horizon to ˙ horizon. No road—no car—no tiny house—no friendly 7-Eleven. Nada. Can't even track back where I could've left the truck and trailer.

Lowers binoculars; stares out.

You ask yourself, how did this come to be? How is it possible? What wild and woolly part of the imagination dropped me here? Makes you wonder.

Looks upstage to horse, back to audience.

Fucking horse.

He hangs the binoculars around his neck by their strap and moves upstage toward horse.

(*To audience, approaching horse.*) Look at that. That's where he winds up. Snorts a chunk of oats down his pipe, straight into the lung, and wham! That's it. End of the day, he's at the checkout counter. Gasping, wheezing like an old fart. Staggering—dead. Barely even got started on the grand sojourn and he drops out from underneath me.

He kicks the horse in the belly, then climbs up on its rib cage and sits on the horse, staring out toward the audience. He picks up the binoculars and scans again.

(*Binoculars to eyes.*) You try tracking it back in your raggedy mind to the original notion—the "Eureka" of it. You remember the moment very clearly—how it came to you. Surprising—"AUTHENTICITY." That's what you come up with—the quest for "AUTHENTIC-ITY." As though that were some kind of holy mission in itself.

Lowers binoculars, stares out.

How could that be? A haunted, ghostly idea to me anymore. At least nowadays—days with age hanging off me like dry moss. Maybe always, I don't know. Far back as I can remember. Some idea—weighing the true against the false. Measuring, calculating—as though you were ever rock-solid certain—as though you ever had the faintest clue.

Stops himself. Listens. Pause.

(*To himself, different voice.*) And who is it exactly you're supposed to be appealing to now? Huh? Who? THERE'S NOBODY OUT THERE! Nobody. Do you see anybody?

He looks through the binoculars. His voice shifts back and forth through this next sequence as though it were a dia-logue between two personas.

No.

Do you hear anybody?

 Lowers binoculars, listens.

No.

Do you have the least little sense of the presence of another being—listening? Listening—

 Pause, listens.

No. Nothing.

Then stop blathering on to yourself, for Christ's sake. What's the point?

Just the sound, I guess.

The sound?

My voice. Hearing my own voice. Me speaking to me.

What in the wide world are you talking about now?

Gives me the impression there's maybe somebody else.

Don't make me sick. Your self is giving your own self the impression there's maybe somebody else?

Something like that.

Who could that be?

I don't know.

You're one sick puppy.

I just need to verify certain things.

Well, do it on your own time.

Sorry.

I've got better things to do than listen to your whining.

All right, all right! Can't we just—

What?

Get along.

Hobart stops himself and looks sheepishly at the audience, as though embarrassed to have been witnessed in this little conflict with himself. He gets off the horse and crosses very deliberately down center, in front of the pit. He talks directly and confidentially to the audience.

All I can tell you is that I had become well aware of my inexorable descent into a life in which, daily, I was convinced I was not intended to be living.

(*Aside.*) This is in the somewhat florid style of the classic narrative. Bear with me. Things will change. It's going to be a long, rough, and rocky road. I'm not exactly sure what "voice" to use. "Voice" in the sense of—you know—what—what voice suits the predicament. The—uh—what predicament I'm actually—it's not at all clear. It's—but hopefully, as things roll along and find their natural—hopefully, something—

He begins to stroll back and forth, extreme downstage, continuing to address the audience.

(*Strolling.*) Long story short, it must have been some other poor fool's destiny I had been assigned to because I couldn't recognize it in any way, shape, or form as my own. Not one drop. Not even the simplest act, like

turning a doorknob or opening the mailbox or address-
ing the doorman by name. Doorman? Oh yes, I had
become quite the big-ass success, no less. No question
about that. Quite the big shot on the block. But somewhere along the trail the thrill of the kill had eluded
me. The *ecstasy* of power—and now there was a kind
of constant hankering for actuality. Hankering? How
else can you put it? The sense of being inside my own
skin. That's what I missed. That's what I missed more
than anything else in this world.

(*Direct to audience.*) How could you lose something like
that?

> *He returns to the self-inquiry between the two voices and
> forgets about the audience.*

(*To himself.*) Are we supposed to reach out now and
somehow walk a mile in your sorry shoes? Now that
you've managed to get yourself into this jam? What is
the petition you're making, exactly? You're not an
immigrant, are you?

A what?

Immigrant.

Why should that be?

You sound funny. Suspicious.

Funny?

Foreign.

I don't know. Maybe it's just the way you're hearing it.

Don't try to put it off on me, now.

I'm not.

Are you the son of an immigrant, maybe?

Probably so. What's the point?

The son of the son of an immigrant? Twice removed?

Twice?

One of those white barbarians Benjamin Franklin brought over to protect us from the Appalachian wilderness?

ABSOLUTELY NOT!

Then what's your story? Why beat around the bush?

Hobart stops. Turns to audience.

(*Directly to audience.*) "AUTHENTICITY."

Pause, then continues to audience:

The little conundrum mounted slowly to a frantic state of crisis. I was running out of time. Birthdays flying by—I could see it coming. I sat down with the wife, face-to-face. Told her—look now, here it is; right here in front of me. I've turned the corner. I can feel it creaking in my bones, my teeth—the eyes are all cloudy in the mornings now. It's coming to get me, I swear. Maybe ten good physical years left and that's it—tits up; roll over, Beethoven. Ten years left to still throw a leg over a horse, like I used to; still fish waist-deep in a western river; still sleep out in the open on flat ground under the starry canopy—like I used to.

Pause, to himself:

When was that? This—"used to"? When was that?

Long pause. He stares out, then begins to stroll aimlessly, kicking at the dirt. He talks to himself and the audience again.

The kids had all flown the coop. Empty nesters—that's us—suddenly. It happens just like that. You don't see it coming. Sitting around, folded up on sofas, sipping tea and reading The Week in Review—the world going up in smoke across the blue Atlantic. Internecine warfare. Remote. Pathetic stuff. Truly. Impotent. What's there to do? I proposed it to her gently, although she had no trouble seeing the sense of it, especially since my nervous condition had gone from bad to worse, constant pacing all hours of the day and night, talking to myself—which is no surprise—and then sudden, unpredictable bursts of fury where I'd rip valuable objects of art off the walls and hurl them out the windows into the lush canyon of Park Avenue: Frederic Remingtons wrapped around the lampposts, for instance; Charlie Russells impaled on bus stop signs, crushed by maniacal yellow taxis. All stuff I'd discovered back in my "truer" days, hanging out worthless in lost Wyoming bars, skunk drunk in Silver Dollar saloons, staring bleary up at these masterful western murals nobody could recognize anymore through the piled up years of grime, tobacco juice, and barroom brawl blood. There they were—forgotten—just hanging dusty and crooked above the whiskey.

He shifts into dialogue voices:

"How much you want for that old cow painting up there?"

"That? Never thought about it. Why would you want to buy something like that?"

"Aw, just to hang up in the tack room, you know. Conversation piece."

"Hell, I guess I'd take twenty bucks for it. Never look at the damn thing anyway, anymore. My back's always facing it."

"Twenty bucks? I'll take it."

Shifts back to speaking to audience directly:

Turned that twenty into a hundred grand, that hundred grand into a million. Whole thing just kinda snowballed. I raided every damn saloon, barn, and attic west of the Missouri—north and south, took truckloads of booty out of that country before anyone even began to take notice. Some of it's hanging in national museums now. What I couldn't see, though, was how those old masterpieces would become like demons, glaring down at me, nostrils flaring, Colt revolvers blazing away. Couldn't see that back then for hell or high water. Things come back to haunt you, that's for sure.

He turns, looks at horse.

Like my horse—this horse right here.

He moves toward the horse.

I told the wife I'd been dreaming about my old horse—the one I'd left behind years before all this success with paintings. I had one good one left, out in the Sand Hills on open range. Course, he was just a colt back then—big, good-lookin' son of a buck, too. Kept visiting me night after night. Just appearing in the dark—standing there with all his tack on—waiting—beckoning with his big brown eyes. I took it as some kind of a sign—some omen or other.

He pauses by the hole and sounds the word down into it—an echo answers back.

OMEN.

He moves back toward the horse.

If I'd known how short he was going to last I'd have thought about it twice, that's for damn sure. Setting off into the Great Beyond with a doomed mount. Look at that. DEAD! Can you believe it? There he is.

nick

He kicks the horse.

And now I've had to dig the gaping hole, of course. Can't just leave him out here to rot in the ragged wind. Let the coyotes and vultures rip him to ribbons. I'm not that callous. Horse served me well, back in the day when work was work. Served me damn well.

Pause. He looks down into the pit.

Been a good long while since I've dug a hole this big, by hand, by God. Back then, of course, I had a spine like a steel rod. Wind and muscle—now—now, it's like every pained shovelful is about to be your last. Every scoop. Pathetic. Got her done, anyhow. Got her good and done. Deep enough to keep the varmints from digging him back up. All that's left to do now is to tip him in and fill it up.

Hobart gets down on his knees and puts his shoulder into the rib cage of the horse on the upstage side, trying to roll the horse over and into the hole. He makes great heaving efforts with no result, as he goes on speaking, breathing harder now.

(*Struggling with horse.*) This is somehow not at all the way I'd envisioned it, back in the planning stage, back in the flush excitement of seeing myself setting out like Lewis and Clark, across the wild unknown. But maybe all it ever is, is blinded by the dreaming of what it might become.

Hobart switches to the stiff front legs, rising to his feet. He shoves on the legs with the same intention but no result. Then, slowly, the body of the horse begins to rotate. Hobart switches to the hind legs and struggles with them in the same way. Again, inch by inch, the horse rotates slightly so that all four feet are finally sticking straight up in the air and the horse is resting on its spine. Hobart continues talking as he keeps changing positions on the horse, going from front to back, shoulder to hip, putting his whole body into it.

(*Struggles.*) Look what became of him, for example—one of them—Lewis, wasn't it? Mr. Meriwether—what in the world was *he* thinking? Shot himself with two pistols in some dark, slab-sided cabin on the Natchez Trace. Imagine that. A pistol to the head and a pistol to the heart. Wanted to make damn sure he was dead, I guess. What was he thinking? To wind up like that—after opening up all that great expanse of country—maybe he realized something. Maybe he foresaw something. Maybe he saw exactly what we were going to do with it. Maybe he did. But me—not me—this is not what I foresaw, for sure. Nothing like this. Some dumb show—struggling with a dead horse, mumbling to myself in front of a gaping hole you've spent a solid day digging, rambling on to imagined faceless souls. There must be plenty out here, that's for sure. Faceless. Not that I require an audience, God knows. Don't get me wrong. I need no witnesses to this—whatever it is. I could just as easy keep it all silent, I suppose, but just the sound of it keeps me company. Voices.

Pause. He listens.

Some sense of company. Other ones, out here. There's got to be some sailing spirits somewhere in all this space. The ones they left behind. The ones that left them and wandered off. Dazed and weaving. Drowned in sand. Skin peeled back like red birch bark. There's got to be some still out there. One or two at least—maybe right here now—floating—gazing down in dismay at this little sad display.

Hobart has wound up exhausted, lying back on the horse's belly, staring up at the sky — the horse's legs stiff and vertical on either side of him, as though cradling him. Suddenly, Hobart snaps himself out of his reverie and jumps to his feet.

There you go, rhyming again! Now you've caught yourself rhyming!

Mocks himself.

"Gazing down in dismay at this little sad display"! Have you got no shame! Who the fuck are you supposed to be now? William Butler Yeats or something? What is the matter with you? This FUCKING HORSE!!

He rushes to the horse and kicks it furiously in the ribs, then stops himself and turns to the audience, somewhat sheepishly.

(*To audience.*) You wouldn't think a common saddle horse could weigh as much as this.

He stares at the horse, which remains rigidly on its spine, legs pointing stiffly to the sky.

Of course, dead weight is famous for being heavier than live. All I need to do is tip him down into the hole there. Just tip him in. Easy enough to say.

He goes to the edge of the pit and looks down.

Bound to be deep enough, don't you think?

(*Looks at audience.*) I'm not climbing back down in there with the shovel, that's for sure. Can't help but feel you're digging your own damn tomb, with the damp walls growing higher and higher all around you, every shovelful. The smell too—the deeper you go. The history of it. The dinosaur bones. Ancient, aching bones. The fossil fuels. All the shit that rolls through your numb skull as you shovel, one scoop at a time. Tedious stuff. You'd be surprised, the way the mind can't sit still—squirming—harking back—leaping forward. Usually always back now, though—rarely forward. No future—not with a dead horse and no prospects but hoofing it out into the Lone Prairie for days on end.

He sounds words down into the hole.

THE LONE PRAIRIE!

He listens to the echo.

What's it come to? What exactly did you have in mind? Intentional exile? What could you hope to find? There's nothing out here. No one! Not a single sorry soul. Look—just take a look.

He holds the binoculars up, stares, then quickly brings them down, in a panic.

I've got to get this horse down in the hole. Now! That's all I know.

He rushes back to the horse in a frenzy and again tries to tip it over into the hole, but the horse won't budge beyond the halfway position. Hobart continues struggling as he speaks.

(*Pushing on horse.*) Fucking horse! Fucking goddamn horse!

Kicks horse.

Look at that! Even dead he won't play ball. Stuck! Hung up. What's the justice in it? I guess I could just leave him. Just turn my back and leave him belly-up, hooves pointed to the heavens. There's plenty others'd do just that, believe you me. Ride a horse into the ground—shoot him for hamburger—eat him raw, some of them. I've known that kind. Yes, indeed. Barbarians.

Pause, puts binoculars up again and scans horizon.

They must have been a desperate bunch—the pioneers—mountain men. Can you imagine?

Lowers binoculars.

All this—space. What were *they* thinking? Just movement—migration—but me—what about me? I'd get out here, on my own, miles from nowhere, and somehow feel miraculously at peace? One with the wilderness? Suddenly—just from being out here, I'd become what? What? Whole? After a whole lifetime of being fractured, busted up, I'd suddenly become whole? The imagination's a terrible thing. No question about it.

Pause.

Well, you can't very well go back now, can you? Tail between your legs. She'd laugh you right out of the house.

Shifts into dialogue voices.

She? You're not going to tell me you're actually missing someone now, are you? The wife? The kids. The Mom. The Dead.

She was amazing to me. She was.

Was?

Is. Still. But then—

In the past?

Yes. In the past. She was beyond belief. I thought I'd died and gone to heaven.

Oh, please—spare me.

She was—

What? Authentic, I suppose?

Beyond—

What's that? What's beyond authentic?

More—more than you can imagine.

Don't make me puke. You put yourself in this situation, now face the music.

I'm just saying—

What?

She—

You obviously can't explain her.

No.

You can't make do without her either. Is that it?

Hobart wanders toward stage-left mound of earth and sits on it, resting, as he reminisces to himself.

I thought I could. I had—in the past. I had been
utterly alone—at other times. Completely. Without
a soul. Not even family. So I know what that was
like. To some extent—but—I mean, I thought I could
handle it. It didn't terrify me anymore. Complete
aloneness. Not like when you're little and—in the
dark, listening—screams—distant—broken glass. Not
like that—anymore. You learn to make do. Make toast.
Little fires. Sing a song to yourself. Hum a little. Still—
I preferred being with her. Really. I did. It was nice.
The companionship. Someone—something you could
depend on. Take walks with. Have tea together. Coffee.
Read the paper. Sleep with side by side. Touch—and
even, talk. Sometimes. Sex. Sometimes. Talk about
whatever—although she loved politics. Liked to get
excited about it. I despised it, so that became—what?
Stale, I guess. Awkward after a while. But we got along.
Don't get me wrong. We became—tolerant, I guess. Of
each other's—what do you call them? Idiosyncrasies?
Yes. That's it. Except for those occasional times when
she'd explode and call me an asshole. Those were the
moments I suddenly realized the depth of her anger.
How much she deeply resented me. Surprising. Time
together does that. Then we'd inevitably go silent.
Sometimes days. A week and a half at most. But then—

Sings in old country western mode:

"Together Again."

Back to spoken voice.

Back to the old routine. Everything forgotten. So you can see how it became hard for me to imagine myself without her.

Suddenly, he leaps to his feet, disgusted with his self-indulgence. Back to dialogue voices:

SNAP OUT OF IT!

What? Sorry—

There's times I don't recognize you at all.

Like when?

Like now, for instance. I ask myself, who is this person I blindly follow? Who's placed me in this precarious situation with no concern whatsoever for my welfare or safety? Who is this dangerous person?

Dangerous?

He laughs.

You can laugh. Have you thought about how you're going to get our asses out of here without a horse?

Our asses?

Yours and mine.

Well—we've got beans enough. Beans enough for a week at least. Bacon. Jerky. Trail mix. Plenty of water. I'm not worried.

He goes to the duffel bag and equipment down right and rummages through stuff.

Glad to see you were thinking ahead.

I'm well prepared for the worst.

You need to trim down.

What?

Trim. Cull. Get rid of some of this extra junk. Looks like a damn yard sale or something. How are you going to carry all of this out of here without a horse? Get rid of it.

Like what?

The saddle, for instance. Toss it down the hole.

The saddle? Bury the saddle?

The horse is dead.

True, but—

Toss it.

Hobart goes to the saddle, picks it up, drags it to edge of pit, hesitates, looks down into hole, looks at audience.

Just toss it. You'll get over it.

Hobart throws the saddle down into the pit, a resounding thud; looks after it, fondly.

Good. Now, the bridle.

He crosses back to the bridle, picks it up, stares at it.

Toss it.

He carries the bridle to the pit, throws it in, again the sound echoes, looks after it, fondly.

Good. Now, spurs.

He crosses to the spurs, picks them up, admires them.

Handmade Garcias. You can't find them anymore.

What're you going to do? Hang them on your blank wall?

He carries the spurs to the pit, throws them in. Sound echoes.

Good. Now, hat.

No!

Toss it.

Not the hat!

Don't be a baby.

No. It won't get in the way.

Make a clean break.

Not the hat!

You're breaking my heart. Toss it.

> *Hobart crosses to the hat, picks it up slowly, considers.*

What about the sun?

It's setting.

> *Lights shift abruptly to a lavish purple sunset, layered deep in scrim, John Ford style.*

What about rain and wind?

You can't predict it.

What about the whole idea?

Which one's that?

The West? The "Wild Wild West."

Sentimental claptrap.

> *Hobart crosses slowly to the pit with hat held out in front of him. He stops at the edge, looks down into the hole, hanging on to hat dearly.*

I—can't.

Do it!

Then what? There'll be nothing left.

The hat can't save you.

But—

What?

The history—

Gone.

No—

Gone.

He suddenly flips the hat into the pit as though afraid to hold on to it any longer. No sound. He turns and looks directly at the audience, then looks back down hole, then back to the audience.

(*To audience.*) I can't believe I just did that.

He looks back down into the hole.

There it is. Down there. I've done it now. Sunk. Separate. Completely separated.

Stop your whimpering.

He looks back toward the remaining equipment.

What else?

Blanket.

He crosses to dark-green saddle blanket, picks it up, turns toward pit, stops, considers.

Don't be an idiot. You remember these nights out here. Ice on your eyelids waking up. Frosty toes. This is no country for the faint of heart.

He wraps the blanket around his shoulders, crosses to pit, looks down into it, looks to audience.

(*To* audience.) There it is. Down there. Gone. In a hole. Gone! Like dropping a bomb—you can't call it back. What a hat that was.

Can the melodrama, please.

There it is. Quadruple X Beaver. Hat like that wasn't made to fall in a hole.

Just leave it. Turn away. Don't keep staring at it like some long-lost love.

Lost what?

Never mind! Just turn away.

He abruptly turns his back on the hat, facing audience. He stares directly at audience, blanket still wrapped around his shoulders.

(*To audience.*) This could really be it now. To lose the hat. It's not a good sign. This could finally be it.

Suddenly the dead horse slams to the ground behind Hobart, back to its starting position, falling toward upstage with a tremendous boom, accompanied by live bass timpani and billowing dust filling the stage. Hobart keeps staring straight-faced at the audience, without turning upstage. Long pause as dust slowly settles. Hobart slowly turns upstage to witness the disaster, blanket still wrapped around him. He studies horse, then looks at audience.

(*To audience.*) Fucking horse. Goddamn!

He turns and moves cautiously upstage to the horse, approaching warily as though it might suddenly spring to life. He gets closer and nudges the horse gently with his toe, then backs away quickly. He does it again.

(*To audience.*) Got a life of his own, that's for sure. That's what I always liked about the son-bitch; just when you thought he was finished he'd jump back up and rope six more steers for you and drag them all to the fire. Tougher than nails.

He nudges the horse again.

Can't say as I blame him, though, for not wanting to go down in the damn hole. Makes you wonder, doesn't it?

He looks to the audience.

Maybe something's watching out for him, something hovering just above the hide. Some guardian angel or other. What do they call them? "Familiars" or "doubles" or—I don't know. More likely they'd be watching out for an innocent horse than a corrupted human. Don't get me wrong, superstition is not my cup of meat. Not to say that I haven't paid attention to it over the years—back when I worked for an honest living. Back in the days of AUTHENTICITY, when I "rode for the brand," as they say: mending fences, doctoring calves, culling cows. Right here, as a matter of fact. Not too far. Out toward Blessing. Valentine. Up past the White River.

"Greasy Grass Country" is what the Oglala used to call it. Crazy Horse was killed right near here, you know. Not too far. Right nearby. Bayoneted to death. Imagine that. Bayoneted. Not unlike Christ, when you come right down to it. Not to mention the two thieves. Spears to the ribs. Sacrificed like some wild beast. Some dangerous critter that might jump up out of the dark and rip your throat out for no reason. That's the kind of fear they had. Tricked him into coming into the fort—starved him right into it—promised him stuff—promised him land—hunting rights—promised him freedom—that's the worst of it. "Freedom" they called it. They were full of promises back then. Still are. Same ones. Crazy Horse—a man of his people. Not many of them left. He was only thirty years old.

He moves to extreme downstage center. The actor drops all pretense of character and speaks from himself, directly to audience, very simply.

Don't you think there ought to be a National Day of Rest for someone like that? A true American Hero. Close the schools. Close the post office. Five minutes of pure silence across the nation. Five minutes of pure silence.

Long pause. He listens intently, slowly raises the binoculars to his eyes and scans the horizon. He begins singing softly to himself, keeping the binoculars up to his eyes.

Oh, didn't he ramble
Oh, didn't he ramble

Rambled all around
In and out of town.

Oh, didn't he ramble
Oh, didn't he ramble
He rambled till those butchers
Cut him down.

As he starts singing the next verse, still scanning with binocu-
lars to his eyes, a Young Woman dressed only in a sheer slip,
and with bare feet, emerges slowly from deep in the pit, wear-
ing Hobart's western hat. He remains unaware of her as he
continues singing. She moves slowly upstage right, away from
Hobart, and stops, gazing out at the horizon line. A very
faint sound of distant prairie wind accompanies the Young
Woman's entrance and remains in the background throughout.

He rambled in a gambling game
He rambled on the green
The gamblers there showed him a trick
That he had never seen.

He lost his roll and jewelry
He like to lost his life
He lost the car that carried him there
And somebody stole his wife.

The Young Woman turns slowly toward Hobart, then moves slowly toward him as he sings the chorus. She stops directly behind him as he continues singing, unaware of her presence.

Oh, didn't he ramble
Oh, didn't he ramble
Rambled all around
In and out of town.

The Young Woman takes off the hat and gently puts it on Hobart's head as he continues singing. She turns away and slowly returns to the pit and descends, disappearing.

Oh, didn't he ramble
Oh, didn't he ramble
He rambled till those butchers
Cut him down.

Hobart stops singing. Lowers binoculars, never having seen the Young Woman. Pause. He stares at the audience. The wind continues in background.

(*To audience, after pause, hat on head.*) Where does the mind go?

Pause. Hobart's eyes shift up toward the hat, aware of it for the first time. He reaches up slowly, feels hat, takes it off and stares at it, then stares out at audience, then at hat again, then turns upstage and stares at pit. He turns back, stares at audience, looks at hat, looks at pit again, looks at audience. He crosses up to pit with the hat in his hands, stares down into it as though questioning how the hat could have reappeared. He looks at audience, looks at pit, looks at hat, then quickly tosses hat back down into pit in the same manner he had originally. He stares down after it, fondly. Pause. He looks at the audience.

(*To audience.*) I can't believe I did that again. I keep doing these things over and over again and nothing changes. This is getting dire. This is getting dark and dire.

Lights shift abruptly to a steely dusk. Distant whistling of prairie wind picks up in the background; it gathers force and some volume as the scene continues. Hobart looks up at the darkening sky.

I've got to get this horse in the ground! Why am I having so much trouble getting this fucking horse in the ground? It shouldn't be this difficult.

He starts toward stage right, looking for his rope.

Maybe you should just leave him.

Hobart stops abruptly. Considers.

What?

Leave the horse. Walk away.

I can't do that.

Goes again for the rope.

He's dead.

I owe it to him.

He picks up the rope and builds a loop in one end, but begins having difficulty, getting it tangled around his legs and snarled up in knots.

(*Struggling with rope.*) We've got to find our way out of here. Find our way back to the road. Where exactly did you park the horse trailer? Can you remember that much?

Hobart drops the rope, picks up the binoculars in a panic and scans out over audience to horizon.

I can't see the road!

It's going to be dark-thirty before you know it.

He panics.

I CAN'T SEE THE ROAD! It's gone! Disappeared!

He drops binoculars, stares out wild-eyed into darkness.

You better build a fire.

No! I'm not spending the night out here, if that's what you think. What kind of treachery is this?

He goes back to trying to gather the rope together, but gets himself even more entangled as he proceeds.

Treachery?

It's as though you're trying to defeat me!

I thought you were self-sufficient. Isn't that what you led me to believe? Entirely on your own. Independent? You don't need my help.

You could be a little more—

What?

Where did we park the horse trailer? Can't you remember?

We?

Me! Us.

How should I know? You were the one got carried away in some reverie. "Right here," you said. "Right here! This is perfect! Pull over."

It *was* perfect.

Then why can't you remember?

I got excited, I guess.

Excited?

Yes.

Like a little boy?

No.

Like a little girl?

Don't be insulting! I got excited about finally taking off into it. About getting here. About—

What?

The Great Beyond!

> *The blanket falls from his shoulders as he gestures expansively to the space.*

Why do you always exaggerate?

I'm not. It was way better than I imagined. For once.

You lost your head.

I didn't.

Then why in the world did you feed him a nosebag full of oats, of all things? Right at the very start.

Making a loop in the rope.

I wanted to—fire him up. Make sure he had enough energy for the ordeal.

You fired him up all right.

I didn't know he was going to suck it down his lung. How was I supposed to know that?

You've lost your touch. There was a time you would have known better.

There was a time! There was a time. Of course there was a time! What's done is done. I'm going to get this horse in the ground and move on. I'm not camping here overnight, that's for sure. It's time to move on. You said that yourself.

Through this, Hobart stumbles to the horse, trips over the coils of rope and tries to untangle himself, sorting out the loops and coils. He goes to the hind feet of the horse and manages to wrap a loop around them and pull it tight. He becomes more frantic and confused as he proceeds.

She'd be fixing supper for you about now, wouldn't she?

Pause. He stops working with rope. Looks out.

She?

She'd be fixing things up, making things cozy. Lighting the lamps.

He goes back to work on the horse, securing the rope.

Stop this constant badgering! What're you trying to do to me?

I'm on *your* side.

Oh no you're not! That's a lie! You never were. You've lied to me about everything. You're a traitor!

You've lost your nerve, is what it is. If you ever had any to begin with.

Stop taunting me! I'm trying to get this done.

Maybe she's gone by now. Did you ever think of that?
Long gone.

He stops work abruptly.

What?

Maybe she's just moved on to another life altogether.

No!

Why not? You're not there.

I'll be back.

Oh, so you're going back now? Now you're going
back?

No! I mean—

Maybe she's run off with another man. A better man.

Stop it! Just stop it!

You never thought of that, did you?

Hobart desperately struggles with the rope. He hauls the slack rope downstage center in front of the pit, the two ends cinched tight now to the front and back legs. He starts pulling and tugging on the rope, trying to rotate the horse up on its spine again, as before. Slowly the carcass begins to cooperate as Hobart rants on.

Just give me a little peace! Can't you? Just a little peace and quiet so I can—just a little cooperation, for a change. Instead of—all the time—I could use a *friend* right about now! Can't you understand that? I don't need some—some—nagging adversary. Some—*why doesn't this fucking horse want to go in the ground?!*

Hobart pauses, exhausted, breathing hard.

Maybe he's not entirely dead.

What?

Maybe there's still some life left in him. Why else would he be resisting?

Pause. Hobart looks at horse, then turns and looks at audience. He drops rope. He runs upstage to horse. Stops, then gives horse a tremendous kick in the belly.

He's dead! He's completely dead.

Leave him, then. Just leave him behind.

No! I already told you. It's out of the question.

Hobart hurries back downstage, picks up slack rope and starts hauling on it again, gradually rotating the horse.

(*Hauling on rope.*) Maybe it's true—maybe I didn't think it all the way through. Maybe I couldn't actually foresee what this whole thing was going to be like— but I'm not leaving this poor old horse out here in the wind and sun to rot away like some forgotten roadkill. He deserves better than that.

Your loyalty is very touching.

Don't patronize me!

No, it is. I'm deeply touched. I truly am. I had no idea you were capable of such kindness.

What's that supposed to imply? I'm not a cruel person. Not—mean-spirited. I've never intentionally hurt a soul.

You keep kicking your horse.

HE'S DEAD! HE'S FUCKING DEAD!!

He throws the rope down in a fury, runs back upstage to horse and starts savagely kicking it as he rants on.

See? See that? Doesn't feel a thing. Doesn't feel a goddamn thing. I can kick him in the head and he wouldn't feel it.

He kicks the horse in the head.

See? Like a block of stone. I can kick him in the neck.

He kicks the horse in the neck.

I can pull his tail. Watch.

He runs to the horse's tail and yanks on it viciously.

Watch this. See this? I can kick him right in the ass and he won't feel it. You see?

He kicks the horse in the ass.

See that? Doesn't even blink. I could kick him in the balls, if he had any. I'd kick him in his fucking——I'd kick him from here to——

A series of frantic kicks all over horse's body.

I'd kick him and kick him and kick him——and kick him and——kick him and——

Hobart collapses in an exhausted heap on the horse's belly, gasping for air. Slowly, he begins to weep softly, head tucked into his elbow. Long pause as Hobart grieves. His arm slowly embraces the horse's belly. He pats the horse softly, strokes its belly. The wind has become more present now, beginning to moan and howl ominously. Very distant thunder, followed by branches of lightning on the horizon. Hobart looks up slowly at the dark sky.

(*To himself.*) So, this is the way you wind up. Not like some gallant bushwhacker but flattened out babbling in the open plains. What the hell did you have in mind, anyway? What was it?

He pats the horse, talks to it.

Maybe the two of us—huh? Maybe that's it. Both of us were meant to go down in the hole. Do you think so? Maybe that's exactly it. Both of us.

He props himself up and looks down into the hole.

Should've dug it deeper.

(*To horse.*) If I was to jump down in there with you, would you be a little more cooperative? Would you maybe be less lonely? Is that it? Just the plain old lonesomeness of it?

He slowly stands, speaks to horse.

I don't expect an answer right away. You can take your time to consider. Just know that at this point—this particular low moment in time—I *am* willing to take the leap. I've got nothing to lose.

Pause.

But I'm not jumping down in there if you chicken out on me. I'm not diving down into all that infernal blackness without getting some assurance that I'll have company.

Pause.

Company—some—warmth.

Thunder and lightning closer. Wind picking up.

(*Looks at sky.*) What're we going to do, huh? Just lay out here and get rained on like a couple of rocks? Drenched to the teeth. You expect me to just hang around here and get rained on while you—

Pause.

No. No, I'm not making any deals. No deals. I'm not bargaining with a dead horse.

He moves down right to remaining equipment, talking as he goes about his business. Searching through the duffel, he pulls out a flashlight, switches it on, finds a small white canvas tent, rectangular, Civil War style and starts struggling to set it up in the semidarkness. Intermittent thunder.

(*To horse, as he struggles with tent assembly.*) Just because *you've* decided to cash in your chips is no reason for me to just—

He turns to the horse violently.

I'm not talking to you anymore, all right? I've had it with you! You and your—dilemma. What about me? I'm out here, wasting my time trying to get you buried and—I'm not buying into this. This is not my first county fair, you know. I can make it through this. I've been through some bitter squalls in my time. Hail the size of baseballs. Freezing rain. Wind that would knock your dick in the dirt, knock you right out of the saddle. This

He waves at the darkening sky.

This is nothing.

The tent collapses; he repeats trying to set it up as he raves on.

This is—this is some little pissant gully wash. Some piss in the oceans—that's what this is. Not enough to turn the dust to mud. I've got beans here! Plenty of beans! Bacon! I've got jerky and trail mix! Shelter! What else do you need? What else?

The tent collapses again; he soldiers on.

A little fortitude, maybe. Vinegar and Moxie! Nothing more than that. Piece of cake! You don't think I've just stumbled out here like some greenhorn tourist, do you? Some SUV nincompoop!

Thunder and lightning closer.

I cut my teeth on this kind of country. Worse! Broke boulders in the High Sierras!

Through lightning and thunder:

Crushed primitive elements! Squashed snakes and scorpions. Right here. Right on this very ground! I'm not just some bumbling fool looking for a handout. Look at these hands! You see these?

He rushes toward the horse, holding out his hands.

Look at these hands!

The tent collapses again; he repeats setup.

You don't earn hands like these backing down from Manifest Destiny! No sir. Not a bit of it.

(*To horse.*) *You*, now—*you* might belong to that tribe of lily-livered weaklings who's ready to roll over and play dead in the midst of monumental challenge, but some of us—some of us are aware of our—

The tent collapses again.

FUCKING TENT!!

Loud thunder and lightning close by. Hobart becomes more frantic in his tent assembly.

(*Struggling with tent.*) What's with this tent? This isn't my original tent, is it? Who ordered this fucking tent? Sabotage and sedition! That's what it is. Why else would I be having this much trouble? Why else? I shouldn't be having this much trouble with— nothing's cooperating. Absolutely nothing. I don't understand it.

Throughout the next sequence the storm becomes more violent.

I do not understand why I'm having so much trouble taming the wild. I've done this already. Haven't I already been through all of this? We closed the frontier in 1890-something, didn't we? Didn't we already accomplish that? The Iron Horse—coast to coast. Blasted all the buffalo out of here. An ocean of bones from Sea to Shining Sea. Trails of tears. Chased the heathen red man down to Florida. Paid the niggers off in mules and rich black dirt. Whupped the Chinese and strung them up with their own damn ponytails. Decapitated the Mexicans. Erected steel walls to keep the riffraff out. Sucked these hills barren of gold. Ripped the topsoil as far as the eye can see. Drained the aquifers. Dammed up all the rivers and flooded the valleys for recreational purposes! Run off all the pathetic small farmers and transformed agriculture into "Agribusiness"! Destroyed education. Turned our children into criminals. Demolished art! Invaded sovereign nations! What more can we possibly do?

Finally Hobart manages to get the tent set up. He climbs inside with the flashlight on. There's barely enough room for him to turn around. He hunkers down, facing audience through the open flap, knees tucked tightly up under his chin, arms wrapped around his lower legs. He is exhausted from his tirade, catching his breath and staring out bleary-eyed. Thunder and lightning crescendo. Lightning silhouettes the dead horse, its legs stiff in the air. Flashlight beam cuts across Hobart's face. Sound of deluge, then weather begins to subside into distance, enough for Hobart's plea to be heard. Darkness pervades.

(*Inside tent, after pause.*) What if I tried praying at this late date?

You? Praying?

"If," I said. "What if."

Don't make me puke. The going gets a little rough and suddenly you're a man of the cloth?

I wouldn't go that far.

An epiphany, is it?

"If"! Is there anything wrong with "if"?

What would you pray for?

A sunny day, I guess. One last bright, shining, sunny day. Is that too much to ask?

What makes you think you deserve it?

Well, there've been other sunny days I never deserved. Gratuitous sunny days where I woke up and they just happened to be there. Beams of light streaming through the window. Her golden hair.

(*Mocking.*) "Her golden hair."

You're impossible to have a civil conversation with.

Well, you're welcome to find somebody else.

   Pause.

So this is it, I guess, huh? "Prominent New York Art Dealer Found Dead in Badlands with Dead Horse. There were no apparent signs of a struggle."

Pathetic.

What do you suppose I had in mind?

Authenticity, wasn't it? AUTHENTICITY.

Oh, yeah.

   Pause.

I think I might try it, anyway. Just for the heck of it.

Try what?

Praying.

By all means. Be my guest.

I've never actually tried it, have you?

Once. It didn't work.

You—put your hands together?

I think it's optional.

Close your eyes?

Why not.

Think—what? Think of God?

Suit yourself.

I don't think I *can* think of God.

Then dream something up.

A bright—shining—sunny—day.

That might work.

The lights bump up abruptly to a bright yellowish prairie daylight. The storm has vanished. Hobart peers out from the tent, squinting his eyes against the brightness. Slowly he emerges from the tent, leaving the flashlight behind. He staggers downstage center, squinting out into the distance.

(*He stops. Speaks out toward horizon.*) Bright. Blinding. Far as the eye can see.

He peers up at the sky, then turns upstage and looks at the horse, still in its rigid, belly-up position, legs pointed straight to the sky. Hobart staggers to the edge of the pit and looks down into it. He sees his hat in the hole. He runs his hand slowly over the top of his head, missing the feel of his hat. He turns to audience. Speaks directly to them.

(*To audience.*) Hat like that shouldn't be down in a hole. Brand-new hat. Hardly even got a chance to break it in.

*Slowly, he climbs back down into the hole where he origi-
nally made his entrance, disappearing. Long pause, then
the dead horse slams forward, this time downstage, with a
mighty boom accompanied by bass timpani offstage, dust
billowing up, filling the stage. The horse falls into the hole
with just its head sticking out. Pause, as dust begins to
settle, then Hobart's voice is heard from deep in the pit,
singing the song as the lights begin slowly to fade to black.
The flashlight remains on, illuminating empty tent.*

Oh, didn't he ramble
Oh, didn't he ramble
Rambled all around
In and out of town.

Oh, didn't he ramble
Oh, didn't he ramble
He rambled till those butchers
Cut him down.

*Lights to black. Flashlight remains on. Music: Dr. John
singing "Didn't He Ramble" from same album, then
lights rise for the curtain call.*

End.

ALSO BY SAM SHEPARD

BURIED CHILD

A scene of madness greets Vince and his girlfriend as they arrive at the squalid farmhouse of Vince's hard-drinking grandparents, who seem to have no idea who he is. Nor does his father, Tilden, a hulking former All-American footballer, or his uncle, who has lost one of his legs to a chain saw. Only the memory of an unwanted child, buried in an undisclosed location, can hope to deliver this family.

Drama/978-0-307-27497-7

TOOTH OF CRIME

Second Dance

An aging rock star in a world in which entertainment and street warfare go hand in hand, Hoss must defend himself against Crow, a newcomer who battles him for fame. Combining musical styles and intense dialogue in an unconventional musical-fantasy, *Tooth of Crime* riffs brilliantly on rising stars and fading legends, and rock lived and died for.

Drama/978-0-307-27498-4

ALSO AVAILABLE:

Cruising Paradise, 978-0-679-74217-3
The God of Hell, 978-1-4000-9651-0
Great Dream of Heaven, 978-0-375-70452-9
*The Late Henry Moss, Eyes for Consuela,
When the World Was Green*, 978-1-4000-3079-8
Simpatico, 978-0-679-76317-8
*States of Shock, Far North, and Silent
Tongue*, 978-0-679-74218-0
The Unseen Hand, 978-0-679-76789-3

VINTAGE BOOKS
Available at your local bookstore, or
visit www.randomhouse.com

ML 6/08